BLACK WIDOW SPIDERS

SPIDERS DISCOVERY LIBRARY

Jason Cooper

Rourke
Publishing LLC
Vero Beach, Florida 32964

www.rourkepublishing.com
1-800-394-7055
Vero Beach Florida

PHOTO CREDITS: Cover, p. 4, 7, 12, 15, 19, 21 © James H. Carmichael; title page, p. 11 © Bryan Reynolds; p. 8, 16, 20, 22 © Mark Kostich

Title page: *A young black widow steps among the threads of an adult female's web.*

Editor: Frank Sloan

Cover and interior design by Nicola Stratford

Library of Congress Cataloging-in-Publication Data

Cooper, Jason, 1942-
  Black widow spiders / Jason Cooper.
      p. cm. -- (Spiders discovery)
  Includes bibliographical references.
  ISBN 1-59515-445-0 (hardcover)
  1. Black widow spider--Juvenile literature. I. Title.
  QL458.42.T54C664 2006
  595.4'4--dc22
                                        2005010726

Printed in the USA

CG/CG

Table of Contents

Black Widow Spiders

The black widow spider is probably the most famous spider in America. It's also the most feared.

The black widow is one of the few North American spiders whose bite can hurt humans. The bite of any widow spider is very painful. A widow bite is not likely to be life threatening, but it should be treated immediately by a doctor. In fact, black widows and other spiders rarely bite anyone.

A female black widow has a bite
than can be dangerous to people.

Widow spiders are closely related to members of a larger spider family, the cobweb weavers. Cobweb weavers spin webs that look ragged compared to the webs of **orb weavers** such as garden spiders.

Widows use webs to catch prey they wrap in silk threads.

Predator and Prey

Spiders are **predators**. They hunt and eat other animals. But they do so with different plans. Widows and orb weavers use web traps.

The widow's web of tangled threads may not get style points from a human judge, but it works. It traps insect **prey**.

Like other web-weaving spiders, widows probably have poor eyesight. They sense vibrations in their web, however. When a trapped insect wriggles, the widow hustles toward it.

A black widow has wrapped its insect prey in silk.

The widow's bite with two fangs injects **venom** into the insect. It might be an ant, moth, cricket, or fly. The venom paralyzes or kills. Meanwhile, the widow has quickly wrapped its prey in silk.

Like most spiders, a widow brings up powerful juices from its gut to mix with its victim's flesh. The digestive juices turn the prey's soft parts into liquid. The widow's tiny mouth sucks the porridge-like prey into its stomach. All that remains of the prey is a hard, hollow skin.

A black widow rushes to wrap up a trapped grasshopper.

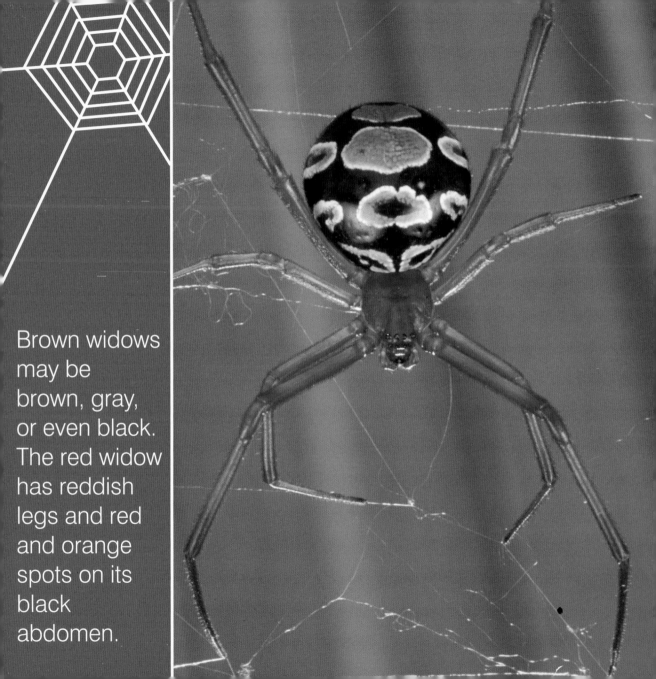

Brown widows
may be
brown, gray,
or even black.
The red widow
has reddish
legs and red
and orange
spots on its
black
abdomen.

Where Black Widows Live

Five widow **species** live in North America north of Mexico. They are the northern black widow, southern black widow, western black widow, red widow, and brown widow. Widows also live in South America, Africa, Asia, Australia, and Europe.

In the United States, brown widows live in Florida and westward into the southern parts of the Gulf States.

The red widow's bite is dangerous, but this spider lives only in Florida.

Widows rarely weave their cobwebs in a home. Instead, they build webs in dark shelters, usually outdoors. Their webs may be under large rocks, logs, or in dirt tunnels. But they also turn up in old barns and outbuildings.

The brown widow shown here with its egg sac is a Southeastern species.

The red "hourglass" on the underside of a black widow is well known. Male black widows often have white trim on their abdomens in addition to red.

What Black Widows Look Like

Black widows are usually shiny black spiders with red or red and white markings. Females are larger than males. Their bodies may be up to one-half inch (1 centimeter) long.

Females are often said to kill and eat their mates. That happens only rarely.

A typical female black widow is shiny black with red trim.

Spiders and other **arachnids** have two main body parts, the **cephalothorax** and **abdomen**. The spider's head, mouth, stomach, and venom glands are in the cephalothorax. Its eight legs are attached to the cephalothorax.

For their size, widows have especially large, round abdomens. A widow's heart, lungs, and silk glands are among the organs in the abdomen.

Widow spiders have large, rounded abdomens.

Black widow males live less than one year. Females may live five or more years.

The Black Widow's Life Cycle

A female black widow lays a mass of some 100 to 500 eggs. She wraps the eggs in a ball of silk, her egg sac. She attaches the **egg sac** to her web.

Black widow spiderlings look like tiny adults except for their color. They may be black, white, or red-striped. They usually grow into adults in two to three months.

Baby red widows emerge from their egg sac.

A male black widow in a female's web stops by his mate's egg sac.

Black Widows and People

Male black widows are not reported to have bitten people, but they certainly can.

Widows and all spiders kill insects, including many that we consider harmful, like fire ants. And like other spiders, widows help keep insect numbers in check.

The smaller male black widows are not often seen.

Glossary

abdomen (AB duh mun) — the second major part of a spider's body; the section that holds heart, lungs, silk glands, and other organs

arachnids (uh RAK nidz) — spiders and their kin; boneless, eight-legged animals with two major body parts and no wings or antennas

cephalothorax (SEF uh luh THOR aks) — the body section of a spider that includes such organs as the eyes, brain, venom glands, and sucking stomach

egg sac (EGG SAK) — a case or container, usually ball-shaped, for eggs

orb weavers (ORB WEEV urz) — any one of several kinds of spiders, most of which spin a flat, somewhat circle-shaped web

predators (PRED uh turz) — animals that hunt other animals for food

prey (PRAY) — an animal that is hunted by another animal for food

species (SPEE sheez) — one kind of animal within a group of closely related animals, such as a *northern* black widow

venom (VEN um) — a poison produced by certain animals, largely to kill or injure prey

Index

Further Reading

Berger, Melvin and Berger, Gilda. *Do All Spiders Spin Webs?*
   Scholastic, 2000
Ethan, Eric. *Black Widow Spiders.* Gareth Stevens, 2002
Simon, Seymour. *Spiders*. HarperCollins, 2003

Websites To Visit

http://kaston.transy.edu/widow.html
http://americanarachnology.org/

About The Author

Jason Cooper has written several children's books about a variety of topics for Rourke Publishing, including the recent series *Animals Growing Up* and *Fighting Forces*.